curious about

CODING WITH DASH AND DOT

BY JILL SHERMAN

AMICUS LEARNING

What are you

CHAPTER TWO
Getting Started
PAGE
10

CHAPTER ONE
Meet the Robots
PAGE
4

curious about?

CHAPTER THREE

Fun with Dash and Dot
PAGE **16**

Stay Curious! Learn More . . . 22
Glossary. 24
Index 24

Curious About is published by
Amicus Learning, an imprint of Amicus
P.O. Box 227, Mankato, MN 56002
www.amicuspublishing.us

Copyright © 2026 Amicus.
International copyright reserved in all countries.
No part of this book may be reproduced in any
form without written permission from the publisher.

Editor: Ana Brauer
Series Designer: Kathleen Petelinsek
Book Designer and Photo Researcher: Emily Dietz

Library of Congress Cataloging-in-Publication Data
Names: Sherman, Jill, author.
Title: Curious about coding with Dash and Dot / by Jill Sherman.
Description: Mankato, MN : Amicus Learning, [2026] | Series: Curious about coding | Includes bibliographical references and index. | Audience term: Children | Audience term: School children | Audience: Ages 6–9 | Audience: Grades 2–3 | Summary: "What are Dash and Dot and how can I control them? Learn about coding, robots, and programming in this question-and-answer book for elementary readers. Includes table of contents, glossary, books and websites for further research, and index"— Provided by publisher.
Identifiers: LCCN 2024048330 (print) | LCCN 2024048331 (ebook) | ISBN 9798892004961 (library binding) | ISBN 9798892005500 (paperback) | ISBN 9798892006040 (ebook)
Subjects: LCSH: Computer programming—Juvenile literature. | Robots—Juvenile literature.
Classification: LCC QA76.6115 .S5282 2026 (print) | LCC QA76.6115 (ebook) | DDC 005.13—dc23/eng/20250117
LC record available at https://lccn.loc.gov/2024048330
LC ebook record available at https://lccn.loc.gov/2024048331

Photo Credits: Alamy Stock Photo/dpa, cover, 1, Howard Lipin/San Diego Union-Tribune/ZUMA Press, 16–17, ZUMA Press, 11; Getty Images/Krystian Dobuszynski/NurPhoto, 13, Lea Suzuki/The San Francisco Chronicle, 2, 4–5, 9, 20–21, picture alliance, 2, 10, San Francisco Chronicle/Hearst Newspapers, 3, 18, SDI Productions, 19; Shutterstock/grapestock, 11, Max kegfire, 14–15, Prostock-studio, 8, sdx15, 11, wellphoto, 7; U.S. Army/unknown, 11

Every effort has been made to contact copyright holders for material reproduced in this book. Any omissions will be rectified in subsequent printings if notice is given to the publisher.

Printed in India

CHAPTER ONE 1

What are Dash and Dot?

MEET THE ROBOTS

Dash and Dot were created by Wonder Workshop in 2014.

Dash and Dot are **robots**. They were made to teach kids coding and technology skills while having fun. Both robots make friendly noises and flash their lights. Dash has wheels and can zip around.

DID YOU KNOW?
Robots may seem modern, but the idea is old. Ancient Greeks, Chinese, and Egyptians all designed mechanical helpers.

MEET THE ROBOTS

What is a robot?

A robot is a special kind of machine. It is **programmed** to do things by itself. Robots may have arms, wheels, or other parts to move and do things like people. Some robots help clean. Some talk. Some even go to space!

Robots make many jobs faster and easier.

MEET THE ROBOTS

Anyone can learn how to code a robot!

Who controls the robots?

WHAT IS BLOCK CODING?

Block coding uses drag-and-drop blocks. Each block is a piece of code. Stack the blocks to create a program! See how different commands move the robots.

You do! Robots can't act on their own. They need **computer code** to tell them what to do. They read the code, line by line. They follow the steps you laid out in the code. Dash and Dot are an easy way to learn about coding.

CHAPTER TWO

How do I control Dash and Dot?

GETTING STARTED

Dash can be controlled using a phone or tablet.

Dash and Dot work with special **apps**! Try using Wonder, Cue, Blockly, Go, or Path. Pick an app you like. Then connect the robots using **Bluetooth**. You're ready to start coding!

SETTING UP DASH

1 DOWNLOAD BLOCKLY FOR DASH

2 PUT DASH ON THE FLOOR AND TURN IT ON

3 CONNECT DASH USING BLUETOOTH

4 ADD CODING BLOCKS USING THE APP

5 WATCH DASH MOVE!

How do the robots know where to go?

Robots don't see or hear like we do. They use **sensors**. Sensors tell Dot and Dash if they are tilted or upside down. They detect sounds. The robots can also "talk" to each other with chirps and beeps.

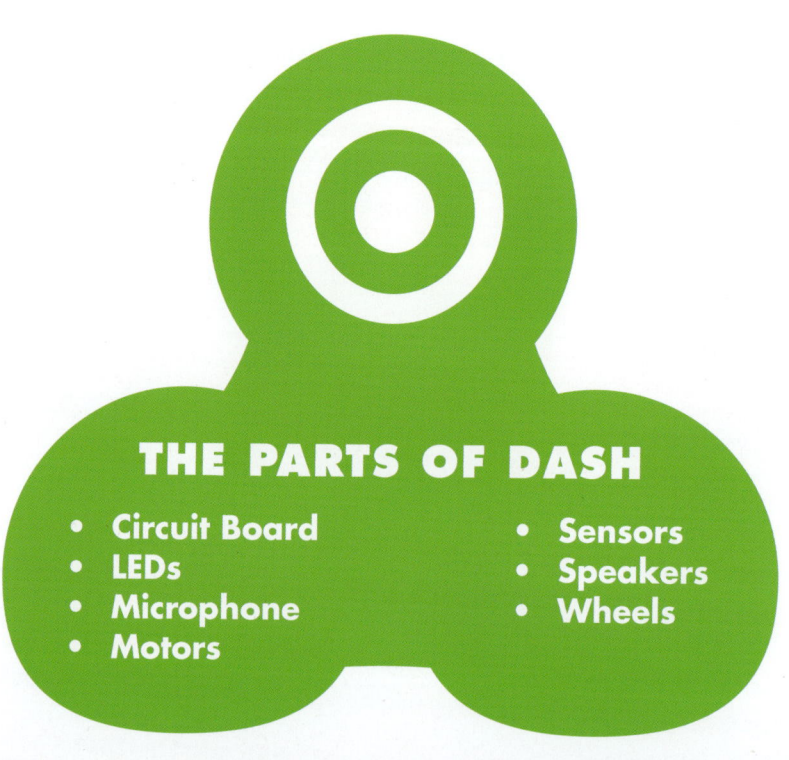

THE PARTS OF DASH

- Circuit Board
- LEDs
- Microphone
- Motors
- Sensors
- Speakers
- Wheels

Dash and Dot can be used to play games like soccer.

GETTING STARTED

Do robots make mistakes?

Ask a parent or teacher if you need help with a code.

GETTING STARTED

Yes! Robots don't always do what we want. It's your job to figure out why. Read the code carefully. Make sure there are no mistakes. Check the sensors. Are they blocked? Make a change. Then try again.

CHAPTER THREE

3

What can I do with Dash?

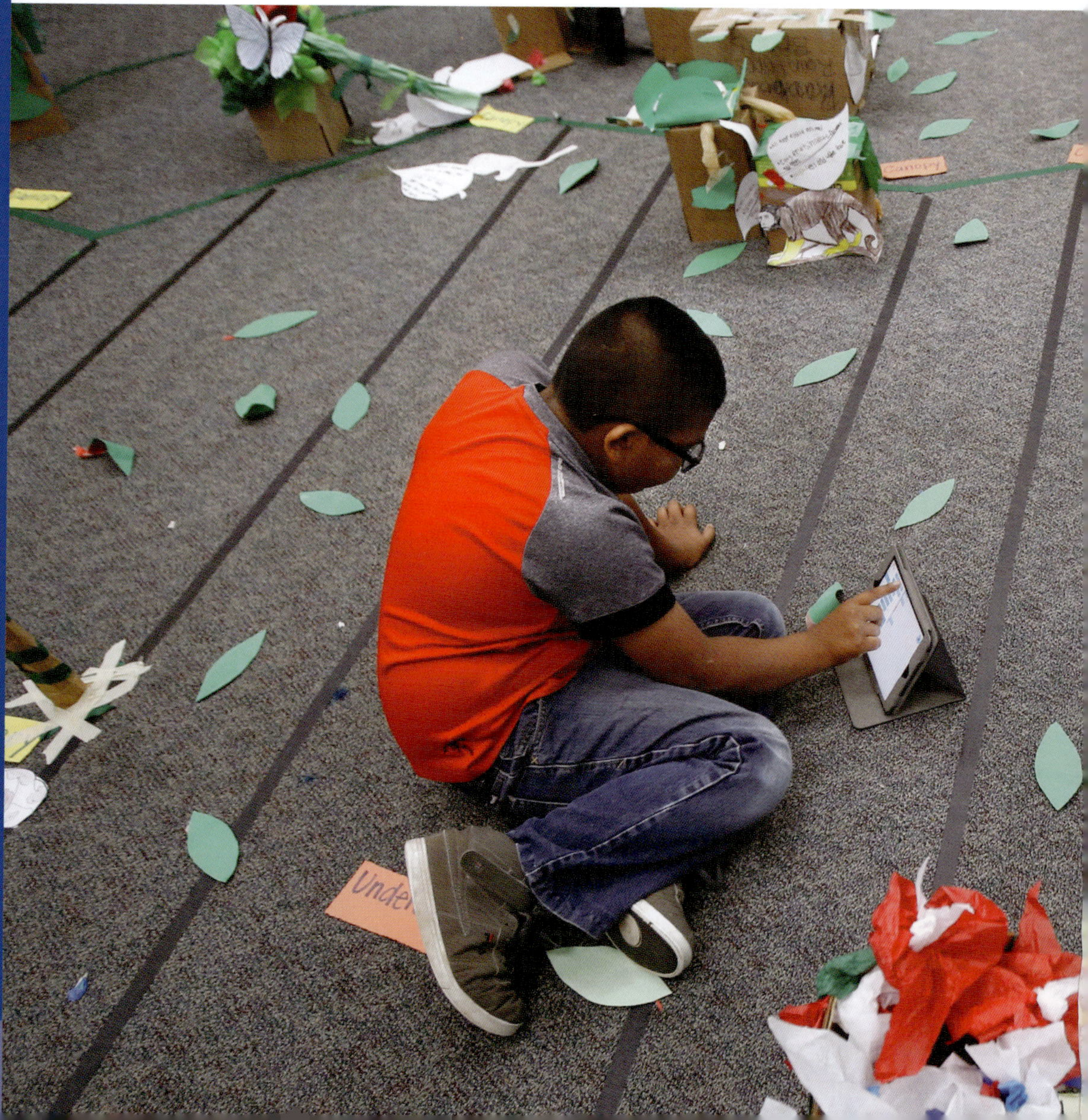

Dash's wheels let it zip around. Put its sensors to the test. Build a maze on the floor. Then program Dash to find its way to the end! Need a dance partner? Have Dash do a dance when your favorite song plays!

This student codes Dash to go through his project about the Amazon Rainforest.

What can I do with Dot?

Dot may not be able to move, but it can still do a lot. Want to keep people out of your room? Have Dot make noise and flash when it spots motion. Want to play a game? Code Dot to turn off at random. Now use it in a game of Hot Potato!

Dot makes learning about code fun.

FUN WITH DASH AND DOT

Can I upgrade my robots?

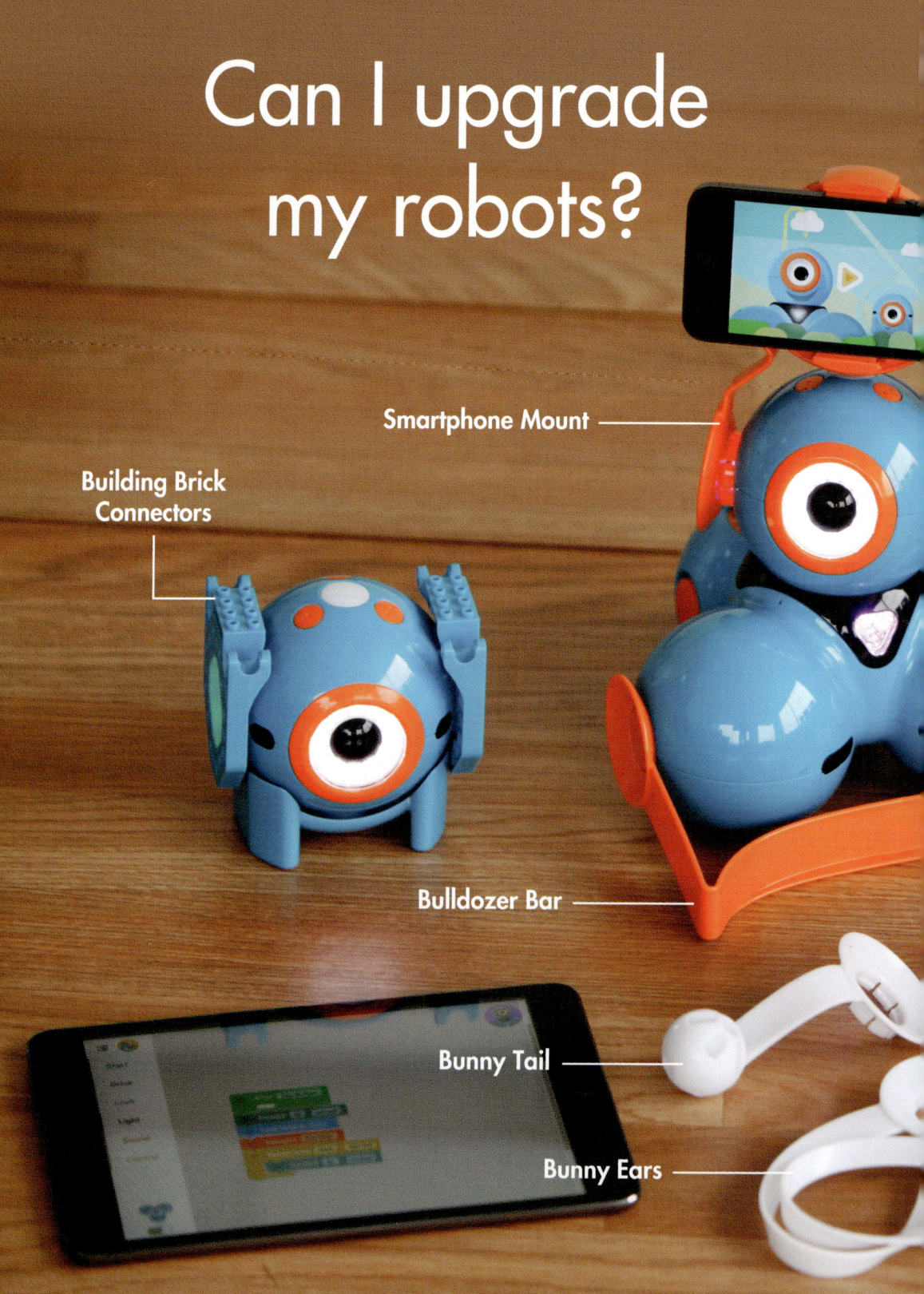

Smartphone Mount

Building Brick Connectors

Bulldozer Bar

Bunny Tail

Bunny Ears

Yes! Special kits give Dash more to do! Add a pair of robotic arms. Now Dash can lift, carry, pull, and place small items. With a launcher, Dash can aim and shoot small balls. What else can you imagine for Dot and Dash?

Xylophone

Tow Hook

Mallet

Accessory kits let you do more with your robots.

FUN WITH DASH AND DOT

STAY CURIOUS

ASK MORE QUESTIONS

How can I build my own robot?

When were the first robots built?

Try a BIG QUESTION: Could robots one day "think" like humans do?

SEARCH FOR ANSWERS

Search the library catalog or the Internet.
A librarian, teacher, or parent can help you.

Using Keywords
Find the looking glass.

🔍

Keywords are the most important words in your question.

?

If you want to know about:

- how to build a robot, type: KIDS BUILD ROBOTS
- about early robots, type: ROBOT HISTORY

LEARN MORE

FIND GOOD SOURCES

Here are some good, safe sources you can use in your research.
Your librarian can help you find more.

Books
How to Explain Coding to a Grown-Up
by Ruth Spiro, 2023.

Robotics
by Nancy Dickmann, 2024.

Internet Sites
Code
https://code.org/student/elementary
Play games and learn how to use block code and control Dash and Dot.

Kiddle: Computer Programming
https://kids.kiddle.co/Computer_programming
Kiddle is an encyclopedia for kids with facts on many topics.

Every effort has been made to ensure that these websites are appropriate for children. However, because of the nature of the Internet, it is impossible to guarantee that these sites will remain active indefinitely or that their contents will not be altered.

SHARE AND TAKE ACTION

Explore some tutorials!
Tutorials are great for learning robotics skills. And they're fun!

Draw a picture of your dream robot.
What would you have it do? Could a robot help you in your everyday life?

Join (or start) a robotics club!
Many schools have clubs where teachers help guide students through projects involving real robots.

GLOSSARY

app A program that runs on a smartphone or tablet.

Bluetooth A wireless connection between devices.

computer code Instructions for a computer program.

program To give a machine instructions to perform an action.

robot A machine that performs tasks for humans.

sensor Something that detects heat, light, sound, pressure, motion, or other things.

INDEX

apps, 10
block coding, 9
Bluetooth, 10
games, 13, 18
kits, 21
parts, 6, 12
robots, 5, 6–7, 9, 10, 12, 15
sensors, 12, 15, 17

About the Author

Jill Sherman writes books about pop stars, baby animals, and robots. She loves that writing allows her to research and learn about new topics. In addition to writing books, Jill sews her own clothes, creates crossword puzzles, and codes in JavaScript.